Advanced Praise

"The poems are beautiful and thought-provoking and speak deeply to the power of the feminine."
— Lindsay Rae, Bestselling Author & Owner of *Self Love Experience*

"Flor did a beautiful job at teaching how to nourish your temple and embrace your glow through her poems on each page. Each time I picked up the book, it really did feel like self-care to me and made me feel more motivated and seen. Perfect if you want to nourish your own temple and really care for yourself through reading."
— Kendall Hope, Author of *Pockets of Lavender*

"This book was really uplifting and magical. Every page gave me a sense of self-reflection and renewal, and I honestly never knew poetry could resonate with me in terms of self-care (mind, body, and soul, if you will). If your first initial thought of poetry is Edgar Allan Poe—like mine was— then I recommend Flor Ana's work 100%, because she's given poetry a new meaning and this journal-like book of introspection is absolutely powerful."
— KaliVictoria, Author of *The Shadows of Heaven*

"With flowery imagery and a dose of spirituality, Flor's poems provide much needed-comfort in a turbulent world. These pages will gently hold your hand as you discover connection in all its forms."
— Marlina Mossberg, Author of *Peach*

"This book is a small investment that will change your relationship with yourself. I often take my copy to the beach or park, connected to nature with a blanket and snacks. It's a beautiful book that gives you a dose of inspiration every time you pick it up. I love the space to journal/draw what you feel. The poems are true, real, and speak to everyone's heart and soul."
— Katerina Rivera, Co-Founder of Infused Karma Artistry

"Flor makes the perfect pairing between poetry and self-care. This collection of poems focuses on enjoying the simple things in life. Reading this collection was a very interactive experience as well as relaxing. The simplistic language and structure of the poems are very well suited to its purpose: to encourage self-care through poetry."
— Jenny Ponce, Host of Miami Lit Podcast

"Amazing read! This is the second book I've bought from this author and her poems always speak to me. Her writing is so divine and calming."
— Stephanie Alfonso, Owner of The Amethyst Boutique

"I absolutely love the concept of this book. Flor Ana created sections for mind, body, and soul. While I already use so many of these self-care techniques, ideas, and nourishments, I found myself drawn to the words she uses to describe the act. Each word is beautifully written, and I appreciated the corresponding page to be mostly blank, but sometimes giving me a prompt to fill in."
— Nikki Chasteen, Assistant Director of the Writing & Communication Center at Nova Southeastern University

*Disclaimer: Reviews have been edited for length and clarity.

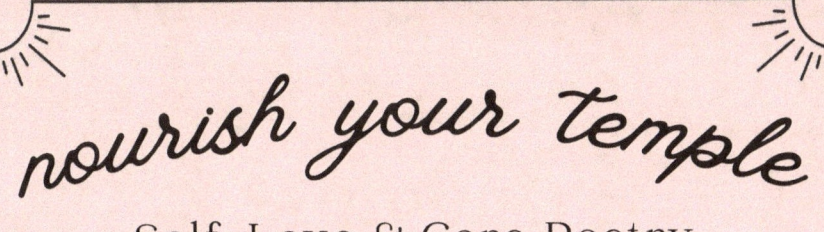

nourish your temple

Self-Love & Care Poetry

Flor Ana

Cover Art Copyright © 2022 by Infused Karma Artistry
Back Illustration Copyright © 2022 by Infused Karma Artistry
Section Illustrations Copyright © 2022 by Raluca Pricop

Edited by Katie Scruggs Galloway

Designed by Indie Earth Publishing

2nd Edition / 02
Paperback ISBN: 979-8-9862106-1-2

For inquiries and bulk orders, please email:
indieearthpublishinghouse@gmail.com

Indie Earth Publishing Inc.
| Miami, FL |

INDIE EARTH
PUBLISHING

"You yourself, as much as anybody in the entire universe, deserve your love and affection."

- Buddha

Dear Reader

First and foremost, thank you for picking up this book. For the casual reader, this may be the first you hear of this book, but for the readers who have been with me since the start, you will notice that this is the second edition of this book, with a new cover, a new title, and many differences in the poems.

I share these pieces of me with you, my thoughts in poetry, to encourage you to give yourself all the love and care you need.

You're free to read this poetry book however you wish—from front to back, back to front—but I recommend let the Universe be your guide. Flip to any random page, read this in one sitting, or a poem every day, or once a week—or whatever you feel you need. At the back of this book is a Table of Contents with all the poems and their page numbers for ease.

Connect with the poem at hand and use the right page to dive deeper. Respond to the prompt or doodle or whatever feels right. Become the co-author of this book. Feel the love for yourself, for Life, the Universe, and everything in between.

At the back of this book, there is also a QR code in case you're wanting to purchase the companion *Nourish Your Temple Oracle Card Deck* that goes with this book.

Enjoy this journey into self-love and self-care.
And never forget, Reader, you are loved.

— Flor

Mind

Burning Bowl Ritual

Fire
a destroyer
a relief
of what once was and no longer serves
a starting anew
releasing the old whose purpose has been accomplished

let us burn and rise
like a Phoenix does in the night sky
let us burn and rise
like a Phoenix does time after time

What are you burning?

Positive Affirmations

Trust the process

Look in the mirror, look into your eyes
Once you look closely,
you'll see the universe inside
and it will remind you
of all the loving connections
and it will teach you
to give yourself affection
because there's only one you
and you're a beautiful soul
so when you look in the mirror
I hope you see yourself whole
and you tell yourself things I know to be true:

I am worthy, I am capable,
I am needed, I am deserving
and I matter too.

Favorite positive affirmations:

Abundance Planning

If life is a series of ones and zeros
may your ones and zeros
bring you abundance
enough abundance
where you can thrive
for as long as you *are*

Plan your abundance
write it down
envision it
the way the ones and zeros
of the Universe
can begin moving in your favor
creating the reality you've always dreamed of

How are you planning your abundance?

Aromatherapy

Breathe in the lavender
and sleep peacefully, relaxed, and relieved

Breathe in the patchouli
and connect with the earth

Breathe in the clary sage
and your mood will be lifted

Breathe in the eucalyptus
and your pain will be eased

Rosewood grounds
and sweet orange will entrance you

calming the chaos that clutters the mind

What scent makes you most calm?

Be Still

Close your eyes
Feel the warmth of the sun on your skin
Hear the chirps of the crickets at night

Be *still*
even if just for a little while
relax and let your worries melt away
tomorrow is a new day
but today
just unwind
reset
relax
give your mind and body a break

Be *still*
and let your senses lead the way

When are you most still?

Sound Healing

music to the ears
brings healing one can hear

an experience of peace
a sway with a melody

cymbals and chimes
a connection to the divine

healing properties of sound
concerts lived fully and loud

all woven through the Universe
found in the humming of the birds
and in the lyrics of a verse

What sounds bring you healing?

Read

traverse worlds at your fingertips

with a turn of a page
and the writing of a sage
you can enter a new world

learn all you can
at the words in your hands
through the stories written down

write your own stories
fiction, poetry, or your tales of glory
awaiting to impact another's life

Reading can take you places
you might have never seen
and teach you of the wisdoms and wonders
you may only find in dreams

What are you reading?

Clean Your Space

Clean your space
put things in their place
find comfort in your own embrace

Feel clean, renewed, and at peace
your mind and soul will be pleased
with what you've done to give yourself ease

Take a deep breath, light a candle and begin
free your space of excess clutter
and let the calm come in

Take time to tidy up.

Deep Breathing

inhale... exhale
let the air you breathe in fill your belly
and with its release
let it blow away
all the stress and overthinking
that fills the mind

inhale... exhale
let each breath grow deeper
aligning you with your calmest self
until you feel whole
and your body feels anew

inhale... exhale
let the peace of deep breathing
show you that no matter what
all will be okay

Inhale... Exhale...
How do you feel?

Make a Vision Board

Manifestations

are a series

of visualizations

only taking

faith and intention

to come to

fruition

What's on your vision board?

Create an Alter

keep an altar in your home
find yourself
gravitating towards it
ground yourself
fill it with *crystals, sage, incense, and aspirations*
find strength in senses
of visions, creativity, love, and admiration

create an altar to create the reality of your dreams

wake up each morning
and decide to be
the best version of yourself
courageous, loving, and full of faith
beautiful, intelligent, and simply brave

How do you stay grounded in your space?

Dream Journal

there must be more
than meets the closed eye
a whole other realm
lies on the other side
one often forgotten
when dreams have done their time

so write down the happenings
or at least what you remember
ponder on their meanings
don't let gold turn into ember

interpret your dreams as you will
but never stop dreaming

What are your dreams telling you?

Meditate

Breathe in...
focus on your breath,
releasing all the stress

Breathe out...
remember, it's okay if your thoughts drift

Breathe in...
remember, this is not about clearing the noise,
reminding yourself *you* are *not* the noise

Breathe out...
once you see the noise is just noise
and thoughts are just thoughts
your mind will begin to clear
and this, this is *meditation*

Meditate for 5-10 minutes.
Write down how you feel afterwards.

Write a Gratitude List

Health
Love
Life
A home
Food
Family & friends
Travel
The ability to breathe
The ability to read
The ability to learn
The ability to be
Everything

no matter what challenges you face
be grateful for life
be grateful for *everything*
because you never know
who's wishing they could be
as lucky as you

What are you grateful for?

Journal

find yourself,
manifest,
come to conclusions

reflect
and see the growth
that the universe has catered

journal at night or during the day
watch as your worries begin to fade

Journal as you need to.

Let Go

L e t   g o
of all expectations and hesitations
that may fill you with doubt and fear.

L e t   g o
of all hate and replace
it with Love, understanding, and compassion.

L e t   g o
of all malice and anxiety
and let the Universe take care of you.

L e t   g o
of all that does not serve you
align yourself with your truth.

L e t   g o
of all that's holding you down and allow
space for ultimate love, life, and revelation.

What are you letting go of?

·Body·

Nourish Your Temple

The Universe has conspired in such a way with all the cosmos to create you. So please don't see yourself as anything other than beautiful, deserving, and absolutely magical. The chances alone of being alive, of traveling through time and space on a blue-green gorgeous floating rock, spinning at roughly 1,000 miles per hour, should be enough to keep you grateful and giddy at just the thought of being human—*flaws, experiences and all. You are the Universe, one and the same.*

How will you take care of your Universe?

Make a Meal

The recipe you saw, stumbled upon
Pinterest, Instagram, or that sits
in a cookbook on your coffee table
follow it

Make yourself a meal that'll make your body feel
good, satisfied, satiated
leaving your taste buds
grateful and tingling

There's something
special,
sacred
about homemade

What do your senses tell you to cook?

Take a Bath

light a candle
let your body sink into the warm water-filled tub
let the peace of returning to the womb
reset your senses and cleanse you

put on music and relax,
focusing on your breath,
sitting still

close your eyes and imagine
the water washing away all the hurt and pain
and when you unplug the stopper,
letting yourself dry
know you've emerged into a new reality

one where you can achieve anything

What are you leaving
behind in the bathwater?

Massage

tensions of the mind manifest as
tensions of the body

allow yourself to relax
allow your muscles to let go of
everything you've been holding on to for so long

undo what has been done with a massage
relieve your stress with intentional touch

worry not
just accept
just be

Trust the Universe always has your back—

massages and all

Allow yourself to relax.

Use Your Hands

use your hands to create
use them to paint
something that reflects how you feel
use them to write
anything that feels right
use them to cook
or read a book
use them to make
something you can take
with you somewhere far
where no matter what
you won't forget how talented you are

What is your Divine Creation?

Exercise

once a week workouts
are the least you can do for your body
the same body that takes you everywhere
and holds your mind and soul

three workouts a week
and you'll begin to see the differences
in your mood, skin and body
you'll feel alive in a way you hadn't before

engage in movement
get your heart pumping
beating
sweat

show up for yourself daily
and trust me when I say
your body will thank you
in all kinds of ways

Create a workout routine.

Dance

Dance

like no one is watching
with the confidence of a thousand suns

Dance

and feel
beautiful and free

Dance

and feel nothing but love
for your own body

What song are you dancing to?

Build Strength

A flower does not grow
with the intention to be beautiful
A flower simply grows
and is beautiful by its own nature

Just like this
you do not build strength
by becoming cold-hearted
instead
you build strength
by being vulnerable
by accessing the winnings and the challenges
the Universe grants you

The flower you are becoming
is beautiful and strong
by simply living life to your fullest truth:
by being yourself, always uniquely you

What kind of strong flower are you becoming?

Drink Tea

The possibility for tranquility lies in tea
chamomile, ginger, black, and green
plus many more that are magical and various
a calming, energetic, or relieving experience

Interpret the tea leaves
for a Universal message to be received
a friend when you need a little something extra to survive
the days, the stress, and tests of time

There's magic in tea
you see
more than just a soothing energy
it's something that holds you

oh

so tenderly

Ask your body what it needs.
Find a tea to meet your needs.

Movement

feel the music
dance with its sway
let its rhythm move you in unexpected ways

feel the waves
ebb and flow with them
the goddess ruling the ocean

feel the movement of your body
heartbeat, pulse, the Universe inside
the moving and growing energy of your mind

feel the movement of your soul
escaping the constructs of space and time
feel it all, feel the divine

How are you moving your body?

Pleasure

masturbation is a form of manifestation
but that's not often talked about

and yet, pleasure isn't just about
making yourself feel good

no
it's so much more

it's
date nights and music
catching up with an old friend
having a self-care day and taking a moment to trascend

there's so much in life to find pleasure in

after all, life and to be alive
are the greatest pleasures we can live

What brings you pleasure?

Hydrate

our bodies are mostly made of water,
yet water may not be our preferred drink
if it means anything, anything at all
bubbly or still in your glass
think of the plants, the flowers, the grass

like you, they need water to grow
because when you give the body water
you give the self the chance to do more
to live healthier, skin looking golden and pure
a chance to have more energy than you did before

Drink a glass of water.
Envision it turning your insides gold.

Beauty Ritual

Beauty is in the eye of the beholder
and even if *you* don't want to see it
I want you to know
you're beautiful
like the flowers that grow
like the clouds against the blue sky
like the Universe itself
because you are the Universe

So engage in whatever makes you feel
beautiful
whatever makes you
happy and vibrant to be in your own skin
because I can assure you
there's no one else like you
beautiful in your own light
shining bright like the moon

What makes you feel beautiful?

Health Checkup

close your eyes
tune into your body, hear its plea
feel your energy

what is your body trying to tell you?

what do you need
to finally feel free
from the turmoil of thoughts and sinking rocks

sometimes drowning your spirit?

you are the Universe,
and as the Universe, you are your doctor
the one person who knows what you need

if only you allow yourself to see

What is your body trying to tell you?
Tune in.

Rest

Take time to rest
to reset
your body and mind
take time
to sleep in,
read a book,
watch a movie,
simply be
still

rest and rejuvenate
rest and feel alive
taking time to rest
is something even done by the divine

Take a break.

Soak in the Sun

rays of light enter through the window
illuminating the room
the warming sunlight brings a yellow jar of happiness
for when you're feeling blue

bask outside,
soak in the sun
let it be nourishment
for when life is coming undone

Have you gone outside today?

Take a Walk

listen to the wind move the leaves in the trees
listen to them whisper:

"come take a walk with me"

walk the woods
feel the grass beneath your feet

solely focus on your grounding
let the forest atmosphere guide you leisurely:

"come forest bathe with me"

listen to the flowers and the bees
returning you to infinity

feel like the mountains or the birds in the sky
all of them singing and flying high

return to Mother Earth
especially if it's been too long
take a walk with her
in case one day she's all gone

Take a walk in nature.
How did it make you feel?

·Soul·

Connect with Youself

when was the last time
if ever
you got to know yourself

the things you like and dislike
what movies make you cry
what books sit dusted on your shelf

take a moment
just for you
to connect

with the person
you are and want to be
take a moment to reflect

what makes you
you
in all senses of the word

what are the things
that await inside
and haven't been heard

How are you connecting with yourself?

Energy Work

The Root:
Never forget your grounding
even when your head is far beyond the clouds
it'll provide security
when you can't decipher the words from the sounds

The Sacral:
Feel all of your emotions
the good, the bad, the ugly and the beautiful
Don't be afraid to engage in intimacy
it will teach you about yourself and others

The Solar Plexus:
Do the energy work, see what you need
then, begin to water your divine seed

The Heart:
Open your heart
even when you've been wronged
find hope and faith within
and most worries will be gone

The Throat:
Allow open communication
and you'll allow yourself to heal
com*municate with yourself and you'll unlock
compassion and creativity*
you didn't know you could feel

The Third Eye:
Follow your gut
let your intuition guide you,
for it will take you far

Flor Ana

This is a sign to simply align.

The Crown:
Find understanding and you will achieve
cosmic consciousness
the ultimate enlightenment

Connect with Crystals

Did you know that crystals are alive?
Bursting with magic and healing properties
Did you know crystals survive almost anything?

Just like you can
if you were to believe in your power

from rose quartz to amethyst and citrine
there's nothing like it
that can make you feel as serene

What crystals are calling you?

Family

bloodlined or bestowed upon by fate
I want you to know that you will always have
family
—even if it's not the people
whose blood fills your veins—

it can be, yet
as the eyes of the Universe
all meant to experience the world differently
family can look differently to us all

in its simplest form
family is what you create
the ones who support you
the ones who want to see you shine
—no matter what—

family are those the Universe wanted you to have
in all lifetimes

Who are the members of your soul family?

Take a moment to tell them how much you appreciate them.

Connect with the Moon

look at the moon
what do you see?
is she *full?*
new?
waxing or waning?

perhaps what you don't notice
is that you're both *goddesses*
both going about
illuminating the night
shining the paths
the Universe set out to follow

next time you look at the moon
even if in the afternoon
remember in *you*
a brightening, beautiful essence, too

What phase of the moon will be out tonight?
Look up at the night sky and see how you feel.

Clear Your Energy Field

sage
palo santo
incense
walk them *barefoot*
through your space
—eyes closed
vibrations rising through your soul—
then
cleanse yourself
sage yourself
align your chakras
and feel anew
ready to take on the world
ready to breakthrough

Feel the vibrations rise through your soul.

Connect with the Earth

butterflies and mushrooms
lizards and flies
the smell of rain
and hot breeze that makes you feel high

it's time to return to mother
she's been patiently waiting
at the park, the beach, the mountains
waiting everywhere while you were creating

it's time to forest bathe
and let your worries wash away
step into nature, breathing it all in
explore the world's wonders for the day

listen closely
to Mother Earth's dearest words

never fear, my love, mother's got you
and I won't ever let you hurt

Flor Ana

How are you connecting with Mother Earth?

Alone Time

bask in yourself and your *me time*
embrace the moments
where you get to be yourself, by yourself

the only person
who will walk your shoes
is you

the only person
to know you on the deepest of levels
is you

so, love yourself and cherish who you are
because, darling, you are made of stuff of stars
and I know
there's no one else like you in the Universe
neither near nor far

How will you spend your alone time?

Connect with Water

Go to a body of water
ocean, stream, lake, river, waterfall
listen to the way
the water moves
the way it *ebbs and flows, ebbs and flows*
forever letting go

If you can't go to a body of water
let one come to you
rain
shower
a drink to hydrate, pressed to your lips
notice how it makes you feel
how it cleanses you
allowing you
to let go, like
oceans, streams, lakes, rivers, and waterfalls do

Flor Ana

Flow like water.

Create Art

Art is beautiful in the eye of the beholder
and you hold inside you
the power, potential and creativity
to create any masterpiece
you decide to embark on a journey with

You hold the capability to
make your life art
beautiful and rewarding to the artist
awing and inspiring to those
who come across you through the cosmos

Create art, make your life the masterpiece
that is you
that is all of *you*

                    you create art and art creates you

What art are you creating?

Chanting

out loud,
repeat after me:

Om, Om
Om, Om
Ham, Ham
Yam, Yam
Ram, Ram
Vam, Vam
Lam, Lam

align your chakras with the mantras
chanting each one, healing from the inside out
see where you feel tension and focus there
chant the mantra that will bring you fresh air

Align your Chakras with the Mantras.

Connect with Your Ancestors

coincidentally
we're all here on this earth
children of the Universe
all part of the human race
tracing back centuries of
bloodlines and traits
traditions and dreams
and just ways of being

never forget where you've come from
your roots and ancestors
because even if they're not here on this plane
their spirits and energies live on through you
so go ahead, make them proud
doing what you know to do best
and that is
always being wholeheartedly yourself

Connect to your ancestral energies.

Intuition

we're told to blindly follow our guts
yet flinch in fear at the thought of the unknown
little do we realize
the Universe is right there with us
telling us

it's okay, you know I've got you

take the plunge
your life will be fruitful

I promise

do not freeze in fear or ignore
what you know deep down to be true

follow your Intuition
let it guide you

strengthen your relationship with self
never forget the possibilities the Universe holds

what you may not be able to see
you will always be able to feel

What does your gut tell you?

Connect with Fire

Fire
the element of
spontaneity
inspiration, intuition
big passion
Living within all of us

We've come from the cosmos
from the earth that has fire at its core
Therefore, fiery spirits reside in us all

Connect with your fire
believe in yourself and
believe in the earth
believe you're in your element
And so you shall be

What's fueling your fire?

Truth

Honestly, honesty looks good on you
because, the truth is, no matter how small the lie
it hurts like the burns of ultraviolet suns
truly unbearable pain.

The Truth,
it sets you free,
bringing ease
even with the honesties
that bring sorrow
because even if they're difficult, tomorrow
is a new day
and you have the power to right your wrongs.

Honestly, honesty looks good on you
so may you always value your truths.

Have you been honest with others lately?
How about honest with yourself?

Look to the Stars

May fate have it that you stumble upon this poem
at night
and if not
may you remember it when you gaze at the stars:

Look up at the night sky
see the flicker and flow of tiny lights
be in awe of the stars
and all that they are
just like you should be in awe of yourself
because like you there is no one else

We are all made of stardust
with souls that will never rust
so when you look at the night sky
remember
you're there
as the reflection of you on Earth
looks up in amazement and stares

What stars do you see out tonight?

Connect with Your Womb

the portal being
how we're all here on this plane
to be a Woman is to be a Goddess
the Creator of Chaos
and the Child of Creativity
bleeding monthly
born anew with each cycle
the Mother, the Creator, the Universe
an embodiment of God with feminine features
with curves and breasts
the Nurturer, the Dreamer
the Doer, the Believer
half of the Cosmic equation
simply Divine

How are you connecting to your feminine side?

Look for Fairies

If you look closely
you're bound to meet a fairy

you'll hear her in a compliment
the way a butterfly flutters in the breeze
the daylight moon
and the whispers of the trees

you'll find fairies
in the breaths of an I love you
in the smile of a loved one
in the flowers on the ground
or in a gifted bouquet
in the food you eat
in the water you drink
in the music that just makes you sway

fairies are everywhere
magic in disguise
and if you look closely, you can find
magic everywhere by opening your eyes

What are your fairies camouflaging as?

Time with Friends

friends are those who believe in you
because they see you as you see them:
equals, all power beings

those who you don't see every day
but when you do, it's like nothing has changed
encouraging you to follow your dreams
helping you get things arranged

friends are those who make you
forget your phone
gaze at space
have deep conversations,
and let you listen to the music they made

those you go out to lunch with
after not seeing them in years
laughing a ton
talking about life and fears

friends are the people you know through and true
the ones the Universe destined to meet you
the ones that will always be by your side
no matter the distance or tests of time
platonic relationships that are always allied

Reach out to a good friend
you haven't heard from in a while.

Music

listen to the music
let the rhythm
move your body
the lyrics
touch your soul
the beat makes you feel
what the musician intended you to feel
listen to the music
use it to heal
approach things in life that once felt surreal
listen to the music
may it make you fearful or cheerful
whatever its lyrics, whatever its tempo
its language always Universal

What are your favorite songs?
Who are your favorite artists?

Plan a Vacation

the world is too big to just stay in one place

e x p l o r e   i t

learn about the customs and cultures
the Universe carefully created
learn how they might differ
from your own life path
or maybe you'll find
beneath the layers of
traditions and tattoos
isms and insights
that we're all the same
just different soul beings experiencing humanness
at the same time

Where to next?

Sing

There's something about singing that
brings about a mood
And, darling, when you sing out loud,
your voice lights up the room
So, sing in public, in the shower, and in the car
let everything that comes with living the music
come and take you far

What is your favorite song to sing out loud?

Contents

Mind

Contents

Body

Contents

Get the companion oracle card deck for Nourish Your Temple:

Inspired by Flor Ana's sacred self-care poetry collection,
nourish your temple, this 30-card oracle deck is meant
to help you do just that: nourish your temple.
With illustrations by cover designer Infused Karma Artistry,
this one-of-a-kind oracle deck features gorgeous designs,
the seven chakras, and inspiring messages, aimed to motivate you to
practice the art of self-love and self-care.

Acknowledgments

This book was originally inspired by Goddess Provisions' *Sacred Self-Care Rituals* oracle deck, illustrated by Tatiana Vedenkina, and my sister who gifted me the oracle deck to begin with. This book has now inspired me to create my own oracle deck, which you can purchase and use alongside your reading with the QR code on the previous page.

I want to thank Infused Karma Artistry for their magical work on this cover and on the oracle cards, and I also want to thank Raluca Pricop for her beautiful section illustrations, which started it all, and Teodora Topor for connecting us. Thank you all for seeing my vision while it was still developing. I want to also give a thank you to Katie Scruggs Galloway for taking the time to read through and edit this book and helping make this book better and Karina Lago for the author photo taken.

I want to thank my loved ones for continuing to support me on my writing journey. I want to thank my family for always showing me love and never letting me forget that I am capable of achieving my wildest dreams.

Reader, I want to thank you for your continuous support, whether this is the first book you pick up of mine or it's your third. Thank you for believing in my words and letting them inspire you. Thank you for all the kindness you've given me. This book is for you. May it help you see the light in yourself that I already see in you.

Lastly, I want to thank Indie Earth Publishing. You've been a dream come true.

If you would like to continue supporting this book, please take a moment to leave reviews on Goodreads and Amazon. Thank you.

About the Author

Flor Ana Mireles is an artist, writer, editor, poet and singer, born in Cuba and raised in Miami, FL. She debuted as an indie author with her poetry collection *Perspective (and other poems)*, which has been called a great introductory book to poetry and "a treasure with each turn of a page."

Flor's second poetry release, *The Language of Fungi & Flowers*, has received praise for its uniqueness and style. She has also edited to the *Stories From The Forest* anthology, which features authors and writers from all over the world. When she is not writing or editing, Flor likes to read, eat, be in the mountains, sing with her band Leather & Lace and, of course, travel. She hopes to inspire more writers and artists and let them know they have the power to achieve their wildest dreams.

You can find her at @littleearthflower on Instagram.

www.littleearthflower.com

More Poetry Collections by Flor Ana

Perspective (and other poems)
A coming-of-age collection of poetry that focuses on keeping the magic, finding yourself, connecting with nature, and opening the eyes to the many different perspectives of reality there can be. There is a tone of curiosity and questioning, as well as a love for life, nature, and oneself. There are poems that focus on family, self-worth, love and growth, and nature.

The Language of Fungi & Flowers
A poetry collection for nature lovers and poetry lovers alike. It explores the symbolic expressiveness of mushrooms and flowers and is complete with colorful illustrations done by Flor Ana herself. While some poems are more personal to the author's life, there's relatability in love, life, and meaning.

Available on Amazon, Barnes & Noble, and more

Signed copies available at www.littleearthflower.com

About the Publisher

INDIE EARTH
PUBLISHING

Indie Earth Publishing is an author-first, independent publishing company based in Miami, FL, dedicated to giving artists and writers the creative freedom they deserve in publishing their poetry, fiction, and short stories. We provide our authors a plethora of services that are meant to make them feel like they are finally releasing the book of their dreams, including professional editing, design, formatting, organization, advanced reader teams, and so much more. With Indie Earth Publishing, you're more than just another author, you're part of the Indie Earth creative family, making a difference in the world, one book at a time.

For inquiries, please email:
indieearthpublishinghouse@gmail.com

Instagram: @indieearthbooks